W9-CHV-592

AUG 13 2002

PUBLIC LIBRARY
DISTRICT OF COLUMBIA

The
Civil War
at Sea

George Sullivan

The Civil War at Sea

Twenty-First Century Books
Brookfield, Connecticut

Published by Twenty-First Century Books
A Division of The Millbrook Press
2 Old New Milford Road
Brookfield, Connecticut 06804
www.millbrookpress.com

Copyright © 2001 by George Sullivan
All rights reserved
Printed in Hong Kong
5 4 3 2

Library of Congress Cataloging-in-Publication Data
Sullivan, George, 1927–
The Civil War at sea / George Sullivan.
p. cm.
Includes bibliographical references and index.
ISBN 0-7613-1553-5 (lib. bdg.)
1. United States—History—Civil War, 1861–1865—Naval
operations—Juvenile literature. 2. United States—History—Civil
War, 1861–1865—Naval operations—Pictorial works—Juvenile
literature. [1. United States—History—Civil War, 1861–1865—
Naval operations.] I. Title.
E591 .S945 2001   973.7'5—dc21   00-041805

3 1172 04824 6052

Acknowledgments

Most of the photographs in this book are from the Mathew Brady Collections at the Library of Congress in Washington, D.C., and the National Archives II at College Park, Maryland. I'm grateful for the opportunity to draw upon these collections and the help that I received from curators and staff members. Special thanks are due Maja Keech, Prints and Photographs Division, Library of Congress; James T. Parker, Archival Research International; and Sean Corcoran, International Museum of Photographs, Rochester, N.Y.

Special thanks are also due Sal Alberti and Jim Lowe for their enthusiastic interest in this project, and for the opportunity to use photographs from their collection of Civil War naval photographs, several of which are published here for the first time. I'm also grateful to Ellen LiBretto for the use of her scarce copy of *Leslie's Famous Leaders and Battle Scenes of the Civil War* (New York: Mrs. Frank J. Leslie, 1896), from which several illustrations have been reprinted; to Judy Bolton and Ann Polito, Louisiana State University; Sally Spier Stassi, Historic New Orleans Collection; Eugene R. Graves, Baton Rouge, Louisiana; and John Kennington, James River Squadron. I also owe a debt of gratitude to Ginny Koeth, upon whose idea this book is based. Thank you, Ginny.

George Sullivan, New York City

Contents

Chapter One

The Civil War at Sea

The Civil War is almost always looked upon as a land war. Bull Run. Gettysburg. Antietam. These are the battle sites that everyone knows.

But the conflict between the states was also important as a naval war. It was a war that was waged on the seas, on inland rivers, and in bays and harbors.

Early in the conflict, the Union Navy's *Monitor* and the Confederate's *Virginia* (formerly the *Merrimac*) hammered one another for several hours in the waters off Hampton Roads, Virginia. The desperate duel, a standoff, signaled the dawn of the age of ironclad warships.

Late in April 1862, Union warships under the command of Captain David Glasgow Farragut steamed into the mouth of the Mississippi River, their guns and mortars booming. They quickly silenced Confederate shore cannons. They destroyed Confederate river ves-

sels. In the end, New Orleans, the biggest city in the Confederacy, fell to Farragut's fleet.

During the war, sleek Confederate cruisers roamed the seas, seeking to capture Union merchant vessels. In June 1864, off the harbor of Cherbourg, France, the Union Navy's sloop-of-war *Kearsarge* caught up with the *Alabama,* the best known of the raiders. In the tense battle that followed, the guns of the *Kearsarge* sent the *Alabama* to the bottom of the English Channel.

The naval engagements of the Civil War may not have been as well known as the land battles. There were fewer of them. They were less bloody. But the efforts of the Union Navy—the blockade of Southern ports, especially—were important factors in the war's outcome.

This book presents a visual record of the activities of the rival navies during the Civil War, emphasizing

Civil War naval battles were often just as harsh as those on land. The Union gunboat Passaic *had its smokestack almost destroyed and suffered these turret dents from enemy fire during the Union Navy's unsuccessful attack on Charleston, South Carolina, in April 1863.* (National Archives/ Mathew Brady Collection)

key battles in which they took part. It is a companion volume to *Portraits of the War: Civil War Photographers and Their Work*, published by Twenty-First Century Books in 1998. That book used dramatic photographs to help tell the story of the war's principal land battles.

This book is not a day-by-day, battle-by-battle photographic history of the Civil War at sea. No such book is possible. In the case of major Civil War naval battles, no photographers were present. They simply did not know in advance where such engagements were to take place.

Besides, there were technical problems. When the Civil War began in 1861, photography was not much more than twenty years old. Taking a picture with a camera was a difficult process.

Most photographic images were produced on rectangular-shaped glass plates. These plates had to first be treated with liquid chemicals. The camera of the day was big, about the size of a television monitor. The chemically prepared glass plate had to be carried to the camera in a special holder. Once the photograph had been made, the plate had to be immediately developed.

Some of these steps required almost total darkness. Photographers working apart from their studios had to take tents with them to serve as darkrooms.

During the 1860s the average person had neither the knowledge nor skill to operate a camera, let alone prepare the glass plate on which the photographic

COURRET HERMANOS
71, Calle del Palacio, 71. LIMA.

When the U.S. Navy's steam-powered sloop Ossipee *called upon Lima, Peru, this young seaman visited a local photographer's studio to have his picture taken. It was printed as a little photograph card, a* carte de visite. *Copies were easy to send through the mail to his family and friends back home. (Alberti/Lowe Collection)*

image was to be recorded. Even in the hands of a skilled operator, a camera of the 1860s was limited in what it could accomplish.

There are no photographs of Civil War ships surging through the water. There are none of sailors climbing rigging or flags snapping in the wind. There are no "action" photographs. This is because making a photograph required a long exposure time, from five to thirty seconds, depending on the amount of light available. (Today, exposure times are measured in tiny parts of a second.) Any attempt to record movement resulted in a blurred image.

Despite the difficulties that they faced, thousands of photographers were active during the Civil War. These were mostly portrait photographers, however. Virtually every town had at least one photographer who maintained a studio and specialized in the likenesses of local citizens. Big cities had dozens of them. Portrait studios in coastal cities were often visited by ship's officers and sailors. They wanted pictures to send home to their families and friends.

When Admiral David D. Porter posed for this portrait at Mathew Brady's studio, a special four-lens camera was used. The result was this photograph, which could be easily cut apart to produce four **cartes de visite**. (National Archives/Mathew Brady Collection)

Cartes de visite had a brownish, or sepia, tone. A dozen could be purchased for from $2.50 to $3.00.[1]

Of all the photographers of the Civil War period, none was better known than Mathew Brady. When the Civil War began in 1861, Brady was thirty-eight, married, and running studios in New York and Washington.

He was also enjoying a reputation as the No. 1 celebrity photographer of the day. President Abraham Lincoln, several earlier presidents, cabinet members, senators, congressmen, and Washington's elite politicians, military leaders, theatrical performers, clergymen, and business leaders had all posed for Brady's cameras.

Brady and other photographers of the 1860s understood the power of photography. They realized that their cameras could be used to preserve history as a visual document. When the Civil War broke out, Mathew Brady made up his mind to become its photographic historian. He wanted to make a complete record of the war's "prominent incidents," as he called them.[2]

Brady did not intend to take the photographs himself. He was the victim of failing eyesight. By 1858 or so, his vision was so poor in fact that he rarely operated a camera himself. To cover the war, Brady hired and

The photographs that they ordered were often produced as little card pictures. Called *cartes de visite*, these took the form of photographic prints that were pasted on a cardboard rectangle measuring 2½ by 4 inches (6.5 by 10 centimeters). In size and form, a carte de visite resembled a plastic credit card of the present day.

Mathew Brady's two-man teams of photographers used horse-drawn wagons like this one in seeking to cover the Civil War's "prominent incidents." (National Archives/Mathew Brady Collection)

While Northern cameramen were covering the war in Maryland, Pennsylvania, and Virginia, photographers in the South were also at work. Most restricted their activities to their immediate area. George S. Cook, based in Charleston, South Carolina, documented the bombardment of Fort Sumter in Charleston harbor. William D. McPherson and "Oliver" (last name unknown), who assisted McPherson, photographed in Baton Rouge, Louisiana, and New Orleans.

In the late stages of the war, Southern cameramen were frequently unable to obtain photographic equipment and supplies. Their output of photographs was cut drastically as a result.

equipped two-man teams of photographers and sent them into battle zones. Each team was equipped with a horse-drawn, canopy-covered wagon that carried equipment and supplies. The wagon also served as a darkroom where glass plates could be prepared and developed.

Early in the war, such exceptional photographers as Alexander Gardner, Timothy O'Sullivan, and James Gibson worked for Brady. At the same time, other of Brady's photographers were making portraits of officers, soldiers, and sailors in his New York and Washington studios.

During and after the war, Mathew Brady assembled an enormous collection of war-related photographs. Only a part of this collection came from his photographers in the field, however. Brady also swapped, bought, or copied thousands of prints made by other photographers. It was usual for him to put his own identification on such prints.

This practice is said to have led to strained relations with some photographers. For example, Alexander Gardner is believed to have left Brady after an argument over the ownership rights to certain images.

Mathew Brady sometimes visited his photographers in the field. On such occasions, the publicity-minded Brady would often arrange to have his own picture taken at the scene of a battle or with troops or officers. In this photograph, taken at Petersburg, Virginia, in June 1864, Brady appears at the center of the scene, wearing a straw hat. (Library of Congress/ Mathew Brady Collection)

Gardner set up his own studio and hired away some of Brady's most talented and experienced photographers.

After the Civil War, Brady fell on hard times. The public was no longer interested in war photos. Sales of Brady's prints dwindled. In addition, Brady had made a number of poor investments. Things got so bad that he couldn't pay his bills. His creditors sued him. Brady lost his New York studio and eventually his gallery in Washington, too.

Throughout these troubled times, Brady managed to keep together his vast collection of photographs. At the end of his life, he was poor and ill. Brady died in 1896. By then, several thousand of his negatives and prints made from them had been purchased by the War Department (now the Department of Defense). This collection was later transferred to its present home, National Archives II at College Park, Maryland.

The Library of Congress in Washington, D.C., and the National Portrait Gallery, part of the Smithsonian Institution, also house major collections of Brady photographs. Other important collections of Brady photographs, assembled by private collectors, are at Harvard University and the Chicago Historical Society.

What is remarkable is that so many Civil War photographs have survived. Many of them are of very high quality. In the case of this book, they offer a striking portrait of the Union and Confederate navies. As historian Alan Trachtenberg has put it, they bear witness to real events.[3]

Chapter Two

Building the Navies

At the start of the Civil War, neither the Union nor the Confederacy was prepared to fight a war at sea. The Union had about ninety ships of various types, but only about half of those were ready for active service.[1] The Confederacy had no navy at all.

As the two opposing sides scrambled to build warships, important changes were taking place in the naval world. Ships had always been built of wood. But wood alone was no longer suitable for warships. In 1861 warships with iron plate had been developed in France and Great Britain.[2]

Ironclads, as they were called, protected against gunfire from enemy ships. They also were able to resist not only cannonballs but projectiles from shell guns, a recent invention. Shell guns fired metal containers filled with explosive charges, usually gunpowder. These projectiles were called "shells" because their metal covering held gunpowder the way an eggshell holds its yolk. When a shell exploded, it could set a wooden ship on fire or rip a hole in its hull.

Another important change had to do with the way in which ships were powered. Ships had been traditionally equipped with sails and driven by the wind. Then came steam power. Robert Fulton designed the first commercially successful steamboat in 1807.

But steam had certain disadvantages. A ship driven by steam needed an enormous amount of coal to keep it going. On a long voyage, a steam-powered vessel needed more coal than it could carry.

Many warships of the time represented a compromise. They were fitted out with masts and sails and powered by the wind. But they also had steam engines,

The gunboat **Galena** *was one of the first ironclads ordered by the Union Navy. When Confederate guns fired upon the ship in June 1862, the vessel was badly damaged. The plates of iron were then judged to be too thin, and had to be removed.* (National Archives/Mathew Brady Collection/James Gibson)

which could be used when a coaling station was close at hand.

Another problem with steam-powered warships was the huge paddle wheel that moved the vessel through the water. Usually located on one side or the other of the ship, the paddle wheel was an inviting target for enemy guns. One well-aimed shot could shatter the paddle wheel, leaving the vessel helpless in the water.

The problem of the paddle wheel was solved by John Ericsson, an immigrant Swedish engineer who, in 1837, invented the screw propeller.[3] The screw propeller was a more efficient means of driving ships through the water. Since it was installed well below the waterline, and thus protected from shot and shell, the screw propeller was a great asset to warships.

To cope with the many problems to be faced in building a strong navy, President Lincoln called upon Gideon Welles, a Connecticut newspaper editor who had been a bureau chief in the Navy Department. Welles joined Lincoln's cabinet as secretary of the navy in March 1861. With a wavy-haired wig and a

Gideon Welles, secretary of the navy in President Lincoln's cabinet. (National Archives/Mathew Brady Collection)

flowing white beard to rival that of any Santa Claus, Welles was the most noticeable member of the Lincoln cabinet. He was also one of the shrewdest.

Early in July 1861, in a report to Congress, Welles stressed the Navy's critical need for ironclad ships. Soon after, construction started on three experimental ironclads. The first of these was to revolutionize naval warfare. The ship, designed by John Ericsson, had no sails. It had no clumsy paddle wheel. Sheets of iron that extended below the waterline protected the ship's sides. The ship had steam engines and a screw propeller. It also had a revolving gun turret that was mounted at about the center of the hull. Ericsson named the craft the *Monitor*.

Built in Brooklyn, New York, the *Monitor* was completed on January 30, 1862. A few weeks later, the vessel arrived in Hampton Roads, Virginia, to challenge the Confederate ironclad *Virginia* (formerly the *Merrimac*). The famous battle ended in a draw. But the *Monitor's* performance convinced Gideon Welles and other Union naval officials that what the Union needed was a navy of monitor-type vessels.

At the time the war began, the Union Navy's greatest pride was its five steam frigates. These were

*Longer than a football field, the steam frigate **Niagara** was the biggest ship in the Union Navy when the vessel went into service in 1857. The ship was assigned to blockade duty off Charleston, South Carolina, at the beginning of the war. (Library of Congress/Mathew Brady Collection)*

huge three-masted, steam-driven vessels, some 275 feet (84 meters) in length. They were looked upon as being superior to any other warships in the world. Their armament included forty 9-inch (230-millimeter) guns. Besides its frigates, the Union Navy also included a collection of wooden cruisers and sloops. Like the frigates, these ships were powered by both steam and sail.

Early in the war, seven ironclads were ordered for service on the Mississippi River. These were flat-bottomed, steam-powered vessels, 175 feet (53 meters) long, with no trace of sails. Their slanted iron-plate sides housed ten 8-inch (200-millimeter) shell guns.

Designed by Samuel M. Pook, these seven ironclads were nicknamed "Pook boats." They were also called "city class" boats because they were named after river

A "gun" was a type of cannon that fired a projectile along a flat plane, like a line drive in baseball. The mortar, a short-barreled cannon, sent its projectile on a high, arching flight, similar to a fly ball to an outfielder. A projectile from a howitzer took a path in between the other "gun" and mortar.

Within these different types of cannons, there were rifled or smoothbore. In the rifled cannon, spiraled grooves were cut within the gun barrel. Rifling improved a cannon's accuracy and gave it greater range—that is, it could fire projectiles over a greater distance.

Cannons were produced in many different sizes. They were often described by the size of the bore, the inside diameter of the barrel. For example, the *Niagara*, one of the Union Navy's steam frigates, was armed with twenty 11-inch (280-millimeter) smoothbores (as well as other guns).

Cannons could also be described by the weight of the projectile they fired. During the Civil War, both Union and Confederate forces used 6- and 12-pounder (3- and 5-kilogram) guns and 12-, 24-, and 32-pounders (5-, 11-, and 14-kilogram) as howitzers.

Captain John A. Dahlgren, commander of the Washington Navy Yard, designed many of the Union Navy's most powerful guns. "Dahlgrens," as they were called, had a distinctive shape. Instead of being tubelike, they were thicker at the breech, the rear part of the gun. Dahlgren guns with 9-, 10-, and 11-inch barrels were installed aboard the Navy's steam frigates. (Library of Congress/ Mathew Brady Collection)

Stephen Mallory served as the Confederacy's secretary of the navy. (National Archives/Mathew Brady Collection)

ports in the Midwest. They included the *St. Louis, Pittsburgh, Louisville, Cincinnati, Mound City* (Illinois), *Cairo* (Illinois), and *Carondelet* (Missouri). In addition to these, several large river steamers were converted into ironclads and provided with heavy guns.

Under Welles's direction, the Union Navy grew fast. From 1861 to 1865, the number of ships jumped from 90 to 670. By the end of the Civil War, the Union Navy ranked as one of the most powerful navies in the world.[4]

To whip the Confederate Navy into shape, Jefferson Davis, president of the Confederacy, picked forty-eight-year-old Stephen Mallory. Born in Trinidad in the West Indies, Mallory grew up in Florida. He was a customs collector in Key West at the age of nineteen. He later had a wide range of occupations. He was a lawyer, real estate dealer, county judge, city marshal, customs collector, and newspaper correspondent.

In 1851 the chubby-faced Mallory was elected to the U. S. Senate from Florida. He served as a senator until his appointment as Confederate secretary of the navy. Mallory made it clear what he intended to do. He would build ironclads. In a report issued on May 9, 1861, scarcely four weeks after the war had begun, Mal-

The Confederate Navy ordered several ironclads such as the **Stonewall**, which was built in France. The ship featured a reinforced iron bow that was meant for ramming—and sinking—wooden-hulled Union warships. (National Archives / Mathew Brady Collection)

lory declared: "The possession of an iron-armored ship as a matter of the first necessity."[5]

Two months later, work began on the hull of the *Merrimac*, which had fallen into Confederate hands at the Norfolk Navy Yard. One of the Union Navy's newest steam frigates, the *Merrimac* was turned into an ironclad fighting ship, then renamed the *Virginia*. As the *Virginia*, the vessel was to play a memorable role in naval history.

That summer, work also began on a number of other warships that were to be similar in size to the *Virginia*. The *Arkansas* and *Tennessee* were to be built in Memphis, Tennessee. The *Mississippi* and *Louisiana* were scheduled for construction in New Orleans.

The Confederacy also built smaller armored vessels to defend rivers, inlets, and ports. About twenty of these were put in service. They ranged in size from the *Albemarle*, which was 139 feet (42 meters) in length, to the *Nashville*, which at 310 feet (94 meters) was the largest of these ironclads.

If ships had been built of wood, the South would have been able to put together a fine navy. But producing vessels that required huge amounts of iron and steel was a problem. The South did not have the factories or rolling mills to produce a large fleet of ironclad vessels. There was also a shortage of skilled labor in the South. Thousands of men in the workforce were taken into the army.

With its production of warships sorely limited, the Confederacy turned to European shipyards. Great Britain, in particular, turned out sleek, fast, heavily armed cruisers for the Confederate Navy. Their mission was to destroy Union merchant vessels. A handful of these raiders were notably successful (see Chapter 6).

Lacking quantity in naval vessels, the Confederacy tried to balance the scales by being inventive. Underwater mines, called torpedoes, were one of their creations. Mines were constructed to float just beneath the surface of the water and to blow up when struck by a ship. Confederate mines sank or damaged forty-three Union ships during the war. Wooden ships were often their victims.

The most notable of all Confederate naval experiments was the *H. L. Hunley*, a submarine named for its inventor. Thirty feet (9 meters) long and less than 4 feet (1.2 meters) wide, the *Hunley* carried a nine-man crew. Eight of these crewmen turned handles that spun the boat's propeller.

At the end of a 200-foot (61-meter) line, the *Hunley* towed a torpedo, a container that held 90 pounds (40 kilograms) of gunpowder. The *Hunley*'s crew was to maneuver the torpedo against a ship's bottom. When the torpedo made contact with the ship, it would blast a hole in the hull.

In its trial runs, the Hunley submerged with ease. But getting the boat back to the surface was a problem. Practice dives usually ended in failure. A test dive on October 15, 1863, claimed the lives the entire crew and Hunley himself.

The boat was refloated and experiments continued. In the harbor of Charleston, South Carolina, on February 17, 1864, the *Hunley* launched an attack against the *Housatonic*, a powerful Union sloop. When the *Hunley* rammed its explosive charge into the side of the *Housatonic*, the warship was rocked from one end to the other by the explosion. The ship quickly sank. The *Hunley* itself was severely damaged by the blast and never managed to get back to shore. So

The Confederates designed and developed containers filled with gunpowder that floated not far below the water's surface. These torpedoes, as they were called, were designed to blow up any vessel that came in contact with them. The torpedoes in this scene are suspended from empty, watertight oil barrels. (Leslie's Famous Leaders and Battle Scenes of the Civil War)

ended the Confederate Navy's experiment with submarine warfare.

While efforts of the Confederate Navy were often quite dramatic, it was never able to mount a real challenge to the Union. In the end, the Union's blockade of Southern ports prevailed. Blockading vessels halted the export of cotton. They stopped the South from importing military supplies. They cut off the South from the rest of the world, and there was little that the Confederate Navy was able to do about it.

Chapter Three

Blockading the South

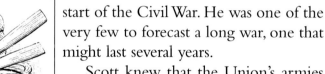

When the Civil War began, Winfield Scott was the general in chief of the Union Army. General Scott could point to a long and brilliant military career. But at the outbreak of the Civil War, he was old, in poor health, and over-weight—too fat to ride a horse, in fact.

Scott had been born in 1786. That made him a year older than the federal Constitution. He had been a hero in the War of 1812. He was acclaimed as a genius during the Mexican War.

Now, at seventy-five, Scott was proud and short-tempered. He liked to wear his formal army uniform, which was adorned with big brass buttons and clumps of gaudy gold braid. He insisted that military rules and regulations be strictly obeyed. This helped him to earn the nickname of Old Fuss and Feathers.[1]

While he may have had some failings, General Scott had a clear idea of his military situation at the start of the Civil War. He was one of the very few to forecast a long war, one that might last several years.

Scott knew that the Union's armies were going to have to attack and invade the South to win. This meant that the Southern armies would be fighting a defensive war. That would make it easier for them. They would be close to home, near their sources of supply.

Because of these realities, Scott did not feel confident about launching a major military effort. He knew that he did not have the manpower that would be needed. His army at the time was tiny, numbering only about 16,000 troops. But Scott had a plan. He wanted to close off every Southern harbor, preventing all ships from entering or leaving.

The South, Scott knew, had very little industry, no means of manufacturing the equipment needed to

Winfield Scott, general in chief of the Union Army in 1861, won President Lincoln's approval for his blockade plan. (National Archives/Mathew Brady Collection)

wage a war. The South was going to have to depend on its European trading partners. By cutting off its sources of supply, Scott's blockade would prevent the Confederacy from achieving battlefield success.

At the same time, the blockade would prevent the South from exporting cotton to England and other European countries. To the South, cotton meant money, the money needed to buy equipment and supplies to conduct a war. The blockade would eventually cripple the South, Scott believed. It also would give the North the time it needed to build, train, and equip a large army.

When the public learned of Scott's plan, he was bitterly attacked. Many Northerners were in favor of sending troops into the South right away. They believed that with a strong and swift attack the war might be over in a matter of months. Scott's plan, by comparison, was looked upon as too cautious. It was even called cowardly.

The Union Army didn't like what Scott was proposing, either. The Army wanted to win the war on the battlefield, with guns blazing and cannons booming. But when Scott explained his plan to President Lincoln, he liked what Scott wanted to do. On April 19, 1861, scarcely a week after the first shots had been fired to open the Civil War, Lincoln announced that in order to protect the "public peace" he was ordering a blockade of all Southern ports.

To make the blockade a reality, Lincoln turned to Gideon Welles, his secretary of the navy. While Welles went about his new assignment with enthusiasm and

The Susquehanna, a sidewheel frigate, was assigned to blockade duty early in the war and later joined in the bombardment of Confederate forts along the Atlantic coast. Here the ship's officers pose on deck in 1864.
(Library of Congress/Mathew Brady Collection)

dedication, he was faced with what at times must have seemed like an impossible task. The Confederate coastline south from Virginia into the Gulf of Mexico covered about 3,500 miles (5,630 kilometers). It offered 180 ports.[2]

The Sabine, an old sailing ship, went on duty for the Union Navy in mid-May 1861 off Pensacola, Florida, which became the first Confederate port to be sealed off by blockaders. (National Archives/Mathew Brady Collection)

The amount of coastline involved wasn't the only problem. The character of the coastline also had to be considered. From Virginia to the southern tip of Florida, the Atlantic seaboard is made up of a series of very long and narrow islands. Between the islands and the mainland are passages of water called sounds. These sounds form an inland waterway along the coastline, which is wide enough and deep enough to provide passage for small vessels.

All a ship had to do to evade the blockade was to slip through an inlet miles above or below the port city, then follow the inland waterway to its destination. To make the blockade effective, it was not enough for the Union Navy to station ships outside the principal ports of entry. The Navy would also have to assign ships to cover the inland waterway.

Finding the ships to conduct the blockade was Welles's first task. He quickly realized that there were not nearly enough vessels available to do the job. And

some of those that Welles did have were the wrong kind. For example, the Navy's powerful frigates and sloops were designed for duty in open oceans, not in coastal waters. They needed deep water. They could not navigate in the shallow sounds of the inland waterway.

With so few warships available, Welles's only choice was to arm about anything that would float. Cannons were put aboard ferryboats and excursion steamers, and tugboats and private yachts. They were put aboard fishing schooners and river sidewheelers. Even retired

(right) In an effort to make the blockade work, sidewheel steamers such as the *Fulton* were pressed into service. (National Archives/Mathew Brady Collection)

(below) This New York ferryboat was purchased by the Union Navy, fitted out with a few guns, and assigned to duty as a blockader. (National Archives/Mathew Brady Collection)

clipper ships were put back into service. Steam- or sail-powered, it didn't matter. Any vessel that didn't leak too badly was a candidate for blockading duty.

Welles and the naval officers he commanded moved very fast. Within a month after Lincoln's proclamation, all major Southern ports were under blockade, except Wilmington, North Carolina. By July 1861, Wilmington was under blockade, too.[3] The blockade was not very effective at first. But month by month, it became stronger.

In time, the economy of the South came to be severely damaged by the blockade. Because of shortages, prices for such items as shoes, clothing, and housewares skyrocketed. The Confederate Army also suffered. Soldiers sometimes had to do without uniforms and blankets. At the Battle of Antietam in September 1862, some Confederate soldiers were already without shoes.

These problems were not caused by the blockade alone. But the string of blockading ships that were posted at each Confederate seaport played an important role in creating the economic chaos that was to engulf the South.

As for General Winfield Scott, he was a mere bystander in all that took place. He retired from active duty on October 31, 1861. Younger officers took over his duties. General Scott made a tour of Europe in 1864 but soon returned to America. He died at the U.S. Military Academy at West Point in 1866. The Civil War was over by then. But Scott died knowing the blockade of Southern ports had accomplished exactly what he said it would.

Chapter Four

Attacking the Confederate Coast

As Gideon Welles began gathering ships to blockade Southern ports, and then started assigning them to their duty stations, he faced a serious problem. For repairs or supplies, or to take on coal, the blockading ships along the Atlantic coast were having to travel to Hampton Roads, Virginia, or to Key West off the southern tip of Florida.

For many vessels, this involved a trip of many hundreds of miles. As a result, some ships were spending more time going to and from their bases than they were on actual blockade duty. There was a simple way to solve the problem: establish more bases along the Atlantic coast by attacking and capturing Confederate ports.

In the summer of 1861, the Union began to do just that. Late in August that year, a squadron of five naval vessels under the command of Flag Officer Silas H.

Stringham attacked Confederate forts guarding Hatteras Inlet, North Carolina. Stringham's warships escorted a pair of navy transports that carried 860 troops.

On the morning of August 28, Stringham's warships opened fire on the forts. At the same time, troops began to land on the North Carolina shore. The Confederates were unprepared for the attack and surrendered the next day.

Hatteras Inlet provided a first-class base for the Navy's blockaders. It enabled the Union to seal off much of the North Carolina coast to ships seeking to evade the blockade. Flag Officer Stringham called Hatteras Inlet "the key to all ports south of Hatteras."[1]

The success of the Union Navy at Hatteras Inlet demonstrated how effective naval guns could be when used against shore positions. The operation also showed that an attack by the Army and Navy together on land

Huge transports landed Union troops at Fort Walker following the bombardment by Du Pont's fleet. They found the fort to be abandoned. (Leslie's Famous Leaders and Battle Scenes of the Civil War)

and sea—an amphibious campaign, that is—could be highly successful. Hatteras Inlet set a pattern for other and similar operations.

Late in 1861, Gideon Welles ordered Flag Officer Samuel F. du Pont to organize a naval expedition to attack and capture Port Royal on the South Carolina coast between Charleston and Savannah, Georgia. A graduate of the U.S. Naval Academy at Annapolis, Maryland, the fifty-eight-year-old Du Pont was a naval commander of long experience. Tall and handsome, he had served in European waters, the Mediterranean, the West Indies, along the South American coast, and the American Pacific coast.

On October 29, 1861, Du Pont's squadron of seventeen warships, led by the big steam frigates *Minnesota* and *Wabash*, left the naval base at Hampton Roads for Port Royal. Forts Walker and Beauregard guarded the harbor entrance to Port Royal. The forts didn't stop Du Pont. He boldly sailed his flagship, the *Wabash*, followed by several other vessels, past the forts. When the forts opened fire, Du Pont's ships answered back.

Once his squadron had passed the forts, Du Pont ordered them to reverse course so that they could hammer the forts again. Du Pont was about to loop around and pound the forts a third time, when he was brought word that the Confederates had abandoned Fort Walker. Later in the day, the Confederates also gave up Fort Beauregard.

With Port Royal in Union hands, the Navy now had another secure base from which blockading vessels

Eight crew members aboard Du Pont's ships were killed during the attack on Port Royal. They were buried at Hilton Head, South Carolina. (Library of Congress/ Mathew Brady Collection/Timothy O'Sullivan)

After the surrender of Port Royal, Timothy O'Sullivan photographed the wharf at the Crosaw Ferry, the ferry that served Port Royal Island. (Library of Congress/Mathew Brady Collection/Timothy O'Sullivan)

could operate. Du Pont received the thanks of Congress. He was later advanced to the rank of rear admiral.

In March 1862, Union forces occupied St. Augustine and Jacksonville in Florida. Fort Pulaski, a harbor fort at the mouth of the Savannah River that protected the city of Savannah, was captured in mid-April.[2]

The ruins inside Fort Pulaski, photographed by Timothy O'Sullivan in April 1862. Fort Pulaski defended the port of Savannah, Georgia. (Library of Congress/Mathew Brady Collection/Timothy O'Sullivan)

Born in New York City in the early 1840s, Timothy O'Sullivan began working in Mathew Brady's New York studio as a teenager. A slender man, quiet and restless, he went on to become one of the most active and respected of all Civil War photographers. Early in the conflict, he photographed near Port Royal, South Carolina, and the islands off the South Carolina coast. He made pictures of the battlefield dead at Gettysburg and took photographs of Union gun crews at Fredericksburg while under Confederate fire. Twice he had cameras knocked out of his hand by shell fire. After the war, he continued to be active, photographing the unexplored American West. O'Sullivan died in 1882.

The early months of 1862 brought other victories for Union forces in Confederate coastal waters. An amphibious expedition into the North Carolina sounds led to the capture of Roanoke Island. Then Elizabeth City and New Bern, both in North Carolina, were seized. After the capture of New Bern, Beaufort and Morehead City, also in North Carolina, were taken.

By mid-1862, the blockade was almost fully established along the southern Atlantic coast. Wilmington, North Carolina, and Charleston, South Carolina, were the only important ports that remained in Confederate hands.

As the blockade got tighter and tighter, so did the practice of blockade-running. Small coastal vessels would take on cargo in nearby foreign ports and then make a quick dash for a Southern harbor. Bermuda was one of the foreign countries used by the blockade-runners. Bermuda is about 675 miles (1,086 kilometers) from Wilmington, and 775 miles (1,250 kilometers) from Charleston.

*The **Colonel Lamb** was one of the best known of the blockade-runners. The steel-hulled vessel ran the blockade several times and was never captured. (Alberti/Lowe Collection)*

Early in July 1862, the Union gunboat Maratanza fired upon and captured the Teaser, a blockade-runner. Damage to the Teaser's deck is shown in this photograph. (Library of Congress/Mathew Brady Collection/James Gibson)

The cotton or other goods were unloaded and shipped to England. Then the cycle began again.

Some of the captains of British vessels looked upon blockade-running as "rollicking good fun." But to sailors aboard Union ships, blockade duty was hard work. Lookouts and gun crews stood for hours at their posts, watching and waiting. One described the routine as "pretty stupid." To another the boredom was "perfect hell."[4].

Profits were high for merchants who dealt in blockade-running. It became worthwhile to build specially designed runners. These vessels were sleek and very fast so that they could outrun blockading ships. They also were built to operate in shallow coastal waters.

As the runners became faster and more elusive, so did the Navy's skill and determination in stopping them. Ships were built that were fast enough to catch the runners. Dozens were captured or destroyed.

To further frustrate the blockade-runners, the Navy stepped up its campaign of attacking and occupying Confederate coastal cities. As one port after another came under Union control, the South slowly strangled.

Large ships would be loaded in England. They would then sail for Bermuda. There the cargo was transferred to blockade-runners, which would immediately set out for Wilmington or Charleston. When the runners arrived in an American port, their cargo was sold. Each runner took on a load of cotton or perhaps tobacco. Dockworkers jammed the cotton bales so closely together in the ships' holds or on their decks that "a mouse could hardly find room to hide."[3] The fully loaded blockade-runner returned to Bermuda.

Chapter Five

Battle of the Ironclads

Of all the ships in the Union Navy at the time of the Civil War, none was more highly prized than the *Merrimac*. Both steam- and sail-powered, the *Merrimac*, with its forty guns and 325-man crew was one of the mightiest warships in the world.

When the vessel went into service in 1854, it had been given the name *Merrimack*. But through the years, the *k* at the end of the ship's name had become lost. Everyone now referred to the ship as the *Merrimac*. The spelling was even used in official documents.[1]

Before the Civil War, the *Merrimac* had completed a long tour of duty in the Pacific. Once the vessel returned to the United States, it put in at the Norfolk (Virginia) Navy Yard. There the *Merrimac*'s engines were to be overhauled.

The *Merrimac* was still at Norfolk when the Civil War erupted on April 12, 1861. Within a week, the Virginia legislature voted to take the state out of the Union. Once Virginia seceded, the Navy Yard at Norfolk was immediately taken over by the Confederates.

Union officers and enlisted men sought to demolish the yard before they fled, setting afire to buildings and ships. Nevertheless, vast stores of food and ammunition and more than a thousand guns fell into Confederate hands. The Confederates also salvaged six ships. One of them was the *Merrimac*.

Stephen Mallory, the Confederate secretary of the navy, ordered that the *Merrimac* be turned into an ironclad. The vessel, which had been sunk in the Elizabeth River near Norfolk, was raised and inspected. The hull was in good condition. Its engines needed only minor repairs.

Work on the *Merrimac* began during July 1861. Workers first cut down the ship's masts. On the flat deck about midship, they built a fortresslike structure with slanted sides of 4-inch (10-centimeter) iron plate.

The naval battle off Hampton Roads, Virginia, on March 9, 1862, between the **Merrimac** *(left) and the turret-topped* **Monitor**. *The violent struggle lasted for more than four hours. (Leslie's Famous Leaders and Battle Scenes of the Civil War)*

Poking through the sheets of iron were ten guns, six 9-inch (228-millimeter) smoothbores and four 6- and 7-inch (152- and 177-millimeter) rifled guns.[2] A 1,500-pound (680-kilogram) metal ram was mounted at the ship's bow below the waterline.

On March 8, 1862, the *Merrimac* was taken out on what the crew thought was to be a test run. But it was not a test. Flag Officer Franklin Buchanan, who had been named the ship's captain, was eager for action. He wanted to attack and destroy the Union ships that were blockading the blue waters of Hampton Roads, a channel, about 8 miles (13 kilometers) wide, at the mouth of the James River just west of Chesapeake Bay.[3]

Buchanan quickly found the *Merrimac* (which had been renamed the *Virginia* by the Confederates) to be a clumsy vessel. The ship's top speed was no more than

4 or 5 miles (6 to 8 kilometers) an hour. It steered poorly; it took a half hour just to turn the ship around. And with a draft of 23 feet (7 meters), it could operate only in deep water.[4]

Even so, the *Merrimac* soon established itself as a fearsome weapon. Buchanan's first targets were the wooden-hulled *Cumberland* and *Congress*, a pair of Union ships anchored near the mouth of the James River. Buchanan knew that they would be easy victims.

The *Merrimac* attacked the *Cumberland* first, ramming the ship and sinking it. The Confederate warship then turned its guns on the *Congress*, setting the ship afire. Around midnight, the burning ship exploded.

Another Union ship, the *Minnesota*, a powerful steam frigate, joined the battle. But the *Minnesota* got stuck in the mud and was not able to offer much help. In an exchange of gunfire between the *Minnesota* and the *Merrimac*, Buchanan was wounded.

It was getting dark. Buchanan ordered the *Merrimac* to head back to its anchorage. He planned to return the next day and finish off the *Minnesota*.

When news of the Confederate ironclad's performance reached the Union government in Washington, it caused great distress. The vessel seemed capable of wiping out the entire blockading fleet, one by one.

President Lincoln asked Gideon Welles what could be done to stop the ship if it decided to come up the Potomac River to Washington. Welles calmed the president by telling him that he doubted that the *Merrimac* could make its way up the river because the water was too shallow.[5]

Early the next day, March 9, 1862, the *Merrimac* chugged out into Hampton Roads to put an end to the helpless *Minnesota* and any other ships it might encounter. As the *Merrimac* drew near to the crippled Union ship, its crew members were distracted by a third vessel, one that looked even stranger than the *Merrimac*. It was the Union Navy's *Monitor*.

The *Monitor* was not a rebuilt vessel like the *Merrimac*. It was an entirely new warship. Designed and constructed under the supervision of John Ericsson, the *Monitor* was not big for a major warship. It measured only 172 feet (52 meters) in length, whereas the *Merrimac* was 263 feet (80 meters) long.[6] The *Monitor*'s deck rode only a foot or two above the water.

Ericsson's creation had features never seen before. The most startling consisted of a revolving gun turret that was mounted on the deck. A steam engine rotated the turret through a full circle. Within the turret, which had been formed of eight

Entered, according to Act of Congress, in the year 1862, by Chas. D. Fredricks & Co., in the Clerk's Office of the District Court of the United States for the Southern District of New York.

Swedish-born inventor and engineer John Ericsson designed the **Monitor** *and the Union Navy's monitor fleet that followed.* *(Alberti/Lowe Collection)*

layers of 1-inch iron, there were two 11-inch (280-millimeter) smoothbores.

Although steam driven, the *Monitor* had no smokestack. The smoke from its coal burning furnaces seeped out through grates in the deck. The *Monitor* was not a fast ship, capable of a top speed of only about 7 miles (11 kilometers) an hour. But it was faster than the *Merrimac*. And it was much more maneuverable than the Confederate vessel.

The *Monitor* had been built at a shipyard in Brooklyn, New York. The "Yankee Cheese Box on a raft," as it was called, was launched on January 30, 1862. A crew of fifty-eight under the command of Lieutenant John Lorimer Worden was assigned to the vessel. The *Monitor* left New York for Hampton Roads on March 6, 1862.

On the morning of March 9, when the *Merrimac* steamed out for a final assault upon the *Minnesota*, the *Monitor* was waiting. As the Merrimac approached, the *Monitor* steamed directly for the Confederate vessel. The *Merrimac* fired first. Then the *Monitor*'s turret spun around and one of its 11-inch Dahlgren boomed.

Shot after shot rang out as the two vessels blasted away at one another. Sometimes they were no more

Two naval officers survey the damage to the Monitor's turret following the battle. This is one of the few photographs depicting the vessel. No overall view of the Monitor is known to exist. (Library of Congress/ Mathew Brady Collection/ James Gibson)

than a few yards apart. Once, the *Merrimac* tried to ram the *Monitor*, but it failed. In the *Monitor*'s turret, the crash and shock of solid shot against the sides stunned the gun crew. Some were knocked to the deck and left dazed.

At one point, the *Monitor* came up behind the *Merrimac* and fired both of its huge guns at almost the same instant. Sailors aboard the *Merrimac* were knocked over by the blast and left sprawled out on the deck, bleeding at the nose, mouth, and ears.

Aboard the *Monitor*, Captain Worden was blinded by a shell that struck the pilothouse. He ordered the *Monitor* to withdraw so he could determine whether

One of the first American battlefield photographers, Scottish-born James F. Gibson joined Mathew Brady in Brady's Washington studio while in his twenties. Gibson is known to have made about 150 photographs of the Civil War. His pictures of Union and Confederate dead at Antietam were among the most poignant images to come out of the conflict. They brought home to Americans the grim reality of the war. Gibson was later a partner of Brady's in his Washington studio, but the two quarreled and the business failed. Afterward, Gibson is believed to have moved to Kansas, although little is known of his later years.

Admiral Franklin Buchanan commanded the **Merrimac.**
He visited Mathew Brady's studio to pose for this portrait.
(Alberti/Lowe Collection)

So ended the most famous naval battle of the Civil War. It had lasted three and a half hours, leaving both crews physically exhausted. Gideon Welles and other Union naval officials in Washington were so impressed by what the *Monitor* had been able to do that they ordered the construction of twenty-one similar ironclads. These were to be steam-propelled, heavily armored warships, with the ability to operate in shallow water. Their guns were to be housed in revolving turrets. They were to be called "monitors."

The *Monitor* itself, and the *Merrimac*, too, both came to unfortunate ends. The *Merrimac* was scuttled and burned by its crew in May 1862 to prevent the vessel from being captured by the Union Army. The *Monitor* went down in an Atlantic storm in December 1862. What remains of the vessel now lies buried in sand in some 230 feet (70 meters) of water off Cape Hatteras, North Carolina. Divers have recovered scores of artifacts from the ship, including its anchor, a mustard jar, and a soap dish from the captain's cabin.[7]

Who won the fierce battle between the *Monitor* and the *Merrimac*? Most historians call it a draw. The North may have come out the better, however. As long as the Union Navy had the *Monitor,* or ironclads like it, the South had no hope of putting an end to the blockade.

the vessel had been seriously damaged. At about the same time, the *Merrimac* also turned away from the battle site. The Confederate ship was leaking and having trouble with its engines.

Chapter Six

The River War

To the South, no city was more important than New Orleans. It was a funnel through which poured all the farm products from the Midwest bound for the Gulf of Mexico and the ports of the world beyond.

Railroads to and from the city led to every other important city in the South. In addition, New Orleans was a manufacturing hub, with more machine shops and shipyards than any other city in the Confederacy.

Union military leaders fully realized the importance of New Orleans. Early in the war, when the blockade was being put into effect, New Orleans was one of the first cities to be targeted.

Blockading the Mississippi was no easy task. At New Orleans, the river divided into three channels, called passes, each of which led to the Gulf. Late in September 1861, four blockaders sealed off the main pass to boat traffic.

This angered the Confederate forces defending New Orleans. On the night of October 11, they sent the ironclad ram *Manassas* and several smaller vessels down the river to challenge the blockaders.[1] The captain of the *Manassas* lined up his vessel to ram the *Richmond*, one of the blockading ships. But the *Manassas* missed the *Richmond*, and smashed into a barge alongside it.

Three of the smaller vessels towed fire rafts. These were flat boats laden with pine knots and other easy-to-burn materials. The fire rafts were set ablaze and released to float down the river. In an instant, each became a floating inferno, the flames reaching high into the black night sky. The swift-flowing river quickly carried the fire rafts toward the blockaders.

Officers aboard the blockading vessels panicked. They ordered their vessels to flee downriver, even though no fire rafts had touched them. In New

Slope-sided ironclad gunboats such as the Carondolet spearheaded the Union Navy's campaign to gain control of the Mississippi River. (Library of Congress / Mathew Brady Collection)

Orleans, the Confederates hailed the encounter as "a complete victory."[2] To the Union, it was a great embarrassment.

The incident upset Gideon Welles, Lincoln's secretary of the navy. New Orleans must be taken, he decided. Welles was aware, however, that the city was strongly defended. The Confederates had the *Manassas*, an assortment of smaller vessels, and the fearsome fire rafts. They also had two heavily armored warships, the *Louisiana* and *Mississippi*, which were in the final stages of construction at New Orleans shipyards.

Even more important to New Orleans's defense was a pair of forts about 90 miles (145 kilometers) downriver from the city itself. Fort Jackson, on the river's west bank, boasted seventy-four guns, including some 10-inchers, the largest of all Confederate cannons.

The smaller Fort St. Philip, on the east bank, was about half a mile upstream from Fort Jackson. Thick layers of sod shielded its brick walls. From Fort St. Philip, some fifty-two guns looked out upon the river.

Each of the forts was manned by about 500 men and well stocked with food, supplies, and ammunition. And each was located at a slight bend in the river. This meant that any ship had to slow down as it approached, increasing the ability of each fort to turn back an attack from the river.

The forts and the ships weren't the only problems. The Confederates also sought to barricade the Mississippi. Several burned-out ships and a number of wooden rafts linked by chains were strung across the river from Fort Jackson. All of these defenses didn't bother Gideon Welles. He still believed that New Orleans could be snatched away from the Confederates.

Admiral David Dixon Porter helped Welles in planning the seizure of New Orleans. After joining the Navy in 1829, Porter had served in the Mediterranean, the South Atlantic, and the Gulf of Mexico. During his service in Gulf waters, Porter had made some thirty trips up and down the Mississippi. His experience would be of enormous value.

Porter and Welles devised a plan that was to be a joint Army-Navy operation. The naval force was to include eighteen warships armed with a total of 250 heavy guns. The ships were to be supported by twenty large schooners that were to be fitted out as mortar boats. Each would carry two 32-pound (14-kilogram) guns and one 13-inch (330-millimeter) mortar.[3]

The Army was to supply 20,000 troops for their operation. Its task would be to occupy New Orleans once the Navy was in control. Admiral Porter was in charge of the mortar fleet. To command the entire operation, Porter and Welles turned to David Glasgow Farragut. Born in Tennessee, Farragut had served in the Navy since the age of nine. He became a midshipman at the age of twelve. He later took time out for school. When the Civil War began in 1861, Farragut was fifty-nine years old with many decades of naval experience.

As his base of operations, Farragut chose Ship Island, an isolated patch of white sand, marsh grasses, and stubby pines. Ship Island was set strategically in the Gulf of Mexico about 40 miles (64 kilometers) east of New Orleans.

When Admiral Porter's mortar schooners made their way up the Mississippi River, tree branches were tied to their masts in an effort to disguise the ships so they would not be recognized by Confederate gun crews at Fort Jackson and Fort St. Philip. (Leslie's Famous Leaders and Battle Scenes of the Civil War)

There Farragut began assembling his fleet. For his flagship, Farragut picked the mighty *Hartford*, a three-masted, steam-powered sloop. Its double-piston engines enabled the vessel to reach speeds of almost 14 knots, or about 16 miles (25 kilometers) an hour.

At Ship Island, Farragut readied his fleet for the battle to come. Tubs of water were placed throughout the ships to be used in putting out fires. Rope ladders were hung over the sides of ships, ready for carpenters to descend to repair damage. Crews were supplied with long metal-tipped poles to be used in fending off the dreaded fire rafts.

As a final precaution, Farragut ordered that anchor chains be draped over the sides of the *Hartford* and other ships. The chains were a kind of makeshift armor, intended to protect each wooden vessel from Confederate shots and shells.

Meanwhile, the Confederates called upon the *Louisiana* to aid in the defense of New Orleans. The yet unpowered vessel was towed downriver and moored

Admiral David Glasgow Farragut commanded Union naval forces at the Battle of Mobile Bay. *(National Archives/Mathew Brady Collection)*

above Fort Jackson. Its guns would join those of the forts in blasting away at the Union ships.

By mid-April 1862, Farragut's fleet was ready to move. The mortar ships headed up the river first. On April 18, they began bombarding Fort Jackson and Fort St. Philip. The pounding continued for five days, during which time the ships lobbed hundreds of mortar shells into the forts.

The forts kept firing back. The shelling from the mortar boats was supposed to silence the Confederate guns and permit Farragut's wooden ships to sail safely past. But it seemed to have no noticeable effect.

Farragut grew angry. He argued with Porter over how effective the mortar fire had been. Finally, Farragut decided he would wait no longer. He would fight his way past the forts, then capture undefended New Orleans. The two forts, cut off from food and supplies, would have no choice but to surrender.

Farragut first had to deal with old ships and rafts that the Confederates had chained together to block the river. Farragut assigned the gunboat *Itaska* to do the job. After revving up its engines to full speed, the *Itaska* plowed into the chains, snapping them.

Two hours after midnight on April 24, Farragut signaled the fleet to get under way. The gunboat *Cayuga*

The mortar each schooner carried was huge, weighing between seven and eight tons. The weapon could fire a cannonball the size of a soccer ball more than two miles. (National Archives/ Mathew Brady Collection)

went first. The other vessels followed in single file. As soon as Confederate lookouts spotted the ships, the forts opened fire. Each ship fired back.

The flashes from the booming guns and towering flames from the fire rafts that had been unleashed lit the moonless night. In the smoke and confusion, Farragut's ships charged past the forts one by one. An officer on the *Hartford* described the scene: "It was like the breaking up of the universe, with the moon and all the stars bursting in our midst. . . ."[4]

Fourteen of Farragut's ships made it past the forts safely. But the *Hartford* was not so fortunate. Off Fort St. Philip, the *Hartford* ran aground while still taking fire from Fort St. Philip's guns. While stuck, the ship was set ablaze by a fire raft. For a time, the vessel seemed doomed, but the crew managed to get the fire under control. With its engines pounding, the *Hartford* shivered and shook, and then slipped free. The vessel quickly steamed out of range of the fort's guns.

By daybreak, Farragut's entire squadron, except for one small gunboat, had completed the daring run and was safely past the forts. Every ship had been hit at least once. Shots and shells had struck the *Hartford* thirty-two times. Among the officers and crew members of the fleet, there were 183 casualties; 37 men were killed, 146 wounded.[5]

When a cluster of cast-iron shot from a gun at Fort Jackson exploded on the steam sloop **Iroquois,** *the explosion killed eight members of the gun crew and wounded seven others. (Leslie's Famous Leaders and Battle Scenes of the Civil War)*

The next day, Farragut's ships sailed up the river to New Orleans, and anchored off the city. At first the mayor refused to surrender the defenseless city, but within a few days he relented. Union troops arrived on May 1 as an occupation force. By that time, Fort Jackson and Fort St. Philip had also surrendered.

With New Orleans in Union hands, the energetic Farragut pushed farther up the Mississippi with several gunboats. He next captured Baton Rouge, about 75 miles (120 kilometers) upriver from New Orleans. Natchez, Mississippi, surrendered in mid-May.

Farragut reached Vicksburg, Mississippi, 400 miles (640 kilometers) upriver from New Orleans, on May 23. Perched on a cliff about 200 feet (60 meters) above the river, Vicksburg was a heavily fortified Confederate stronghold. Although he poured shot and shell into the city, Farragut could not silence Vicksburg's guns.

One of Farragut's worries at the time was the *Arkansas*, a powerful Confederate ironclad. In an awesome display of courage, the *Arkansas* managed to battle its way through Farragut's entire fleet of ironclads, gunboats, river steamers, and other vessels, to find shelter beneath Vicksburg's guns. Later in the year, near Baton Rouge, the *Arkansas* was run ashore and blown up by its crew to avoid capture by Union forces.

Farragut remained at Vicksburg for only a few days, then withdrew. He returned to the city in mid-June. He again pounded the city with gunfire, but Vicksburg continued to resist. Toward the end of July, Farragut received orders to return to New Orleans with his fleet.

Farragut could return with a great sense of achievement. The Union Navy now controlled the entire Mississippi River, except for Vicksburg, Mississippi, and Port Hudson, Louisiana.

Earlier in the year, the Union had scored important victories in gaining control of the middle Mississippi. Some 15,000 troops under General Ulysses S. Grant, aided by gunboats commanded by Admiral Andrew Foote, captured Fort Henry and Fort Donelson in Tennessee. Foote's gunboats were also vital in the capture of Island No. 10, a Confederate strongpoint in the Mississippi River near the Kentucky-Tennessee border. (Island No. 10 was so named because it was the tenth island in the Mississippi River south of the point where the Ohio River joins the Mississippi.)

As for Vicksburg, it fell to Union forces under General Ulysses S. Grant on July 4, 1863. At about the same time, the Confederates suffered a stunning defeat at Gettysburg. Less than a week later, Port Hudson surrendered.

Union forces now controlled the Mississippi River. The Confederacy was split in half. Fear and sadness gripped the South. There could be no doubt now as to the war's outcome.

Chapter Seven

Confederate Raiders

When the English-built *Alabama* went into service for the Confederate Navy in 1862, the vessel's commanding officer was given orders to "attack, subdue, scuttle, and take" any Union merchant ship that it could find.[1]

And that's just what the *Alabama* did. Indeed, the *Alabama* was the most successful of all the Confederate Navy's heavily armed warships whose mission it was to seek out, capture, and destroy Union cargo-carrying ships. In the twenty-two months that the vessel roamed the seas, the *Alabama* captured or destroyed sixty-four Union merchant ships, a remarkable total.

Raiders such as the *Alabama*, which were also called cruisers, came into existence partly in answer to the Union blockade of Southern ports. While the raiders' goal was to destroy Union merchant shipping, it was also hoped that Union blockaders would be lured away from Southern ports to pursue the marauders. The blockade itself would thus be weakened.

Although the Confederacy was never able to put more than eighteen or so of the raiders into service, they captured or destroyed 257 Union vessels. Their exploits served as a boost to Southern morale.

Like other raiders, the *Alabama* was secretly ordered from a British shipyard in Liverpool. The Union government protested when it became known that the ship was under construction. After all, Great Britain was officially a neutral nation. As such, how could the British build a warship for the Confederates?

It was possible because of a loophole in the regulations. The basic law stated that any ship built in Great Britain for the Confederacy could not be fitted out as a warship. The British evaded the law by sailing the

*Captain Raphael Semmes took command of the **Alabama** in the spring of 1862 and sailed the raider for almost two years, capturing or destroying dozens of Union merchant ships. (International Museum of Photography, Rochester, New York)*

nearly completed vessel to the island of Terceira in the Azores, located in the Atlantic west of Portugal. There the ship was made ready for duty as a raider.

Built of the finest oak, its bottom clad in sheet copper, the *Alabama* was rigged as a three-masted sailing vessel. But for greater power, the captain could rely on the ship's coal-burning boilers that produced steam for its twin 300-horsepower engines. These enabled the *Alabama* to achieve speeds of up to 13 knots, or about 15 miles (24 kilometers) an hour, which was very fast for the time.[2]

In the Azores, supplies and tons of coal were loaded aboard. Six 32-pound (14-kilogram) cannon were put in place, as were two larger guns. One of these, a Blakely Gun, was a newly designed weapon, capable of firing a 110-pound (50-kilogram) shell.

Raphael Semmes, who had resigned his commission in the U.S. Navy after twenty-five years of service, was named to command the *Alabama*. A small, wiry fifty-three-year-old man, brimming with confidence, Semmes had been born in Maryland and now lived in Mobile, Alabama. He didn't like Northerners—New England Yankees, in particular.

On August 24, 1862, the *Alabama* was put into commission. The Confederate flag was hoisted over the ship. A band played. The crew cheered.[3] The *Alabama* headed out to sea. Off the Azores, Semmes spotted a fleet of Northern whalers. He quickly destroyed several of the defenseless vessels.

Semmes then took the *Alabama* across the Atlantic. For a time he cruised in the coastal waters off Newfoundland, where he captured several ships. Because of the blockade, Captain Semmes could not take any vessels that he seized into Southern ports. He ordered the ships to be set afire, after first removing the passengers and crew and taking possession of any valuable property. The people that Semmes took into custody, who sometimes included women and children, were eventually transferred to a neutral ship or released at a neutral port.

When the *Alabama* needed coal, Semmes set course for Fort-de-France, Martinique, a French island in the West Indies. Semmes then took the *Alabama* west through the Caribbean and north into the Gulf of Mexico. On the way, he captured the *Ariel,* a Union mail steamer bound from New York to California. Aboard were 700 passengers, including 150 marines. Semmes released the ship after demanding and being promised a ransom.

Semmes's next victim was not so fortunate. From Northern newspapers recovered from the *Ariel,* Semmes learned that a fleet of Union transports carrying some 20,000 federal troops was about to sail for the Gulf of Mexico. Semmes believed that the expedition was headed for Galveston, Texas, and he was right.

The *Alabama* arrived off Galveston on January 11, 1863, to find the port guarded by five blockaders. One of the ships, the *Hatteras,* steamed out to get a better look at the *Alabama*. Semmes led the warship out into open ocean, then suddenly turned about and opened fire. The *Hatteras,* a former passenger steamer, was no match for the *Alabama*. In a battle that lasted only thirteen minutes, the *Alabama*'s guns sent the *Hatteras* to the bottom.

Gideon Welles was so angry that he ordered a fleet of warships to pursue the *Alabama*. Semmes was able to

In the North, Captain Semmes was branded as a pirate, and served as the subject for this cartoony drawing. (Alberti/Lowe Collection)

Semmes Motto "I am here"

evade capture by taking the *Alabama* into the Caribbean. At Port Royal, Jamaica, Semmes put ashore the many prisoners he had taken. He also took on coal and repaired damage to the ship that had resulted from enemy gunfire.

Late in 1863, Semmes decided to shift operations to the China Sea. There he hoped to make Union clipper ships his victims. The *Alabama* arrived in Cape Town, South Africa, in March 1864.

The *Alabama* was now badly in need of repairs. The ship, according to one officer, was "loose at every joint."[4] Semmes decided to take the *Alabama* back to Europe to be overhauled. On June 11, 1864, the *Alabama* pulled into the harbor at Cherbourg, France.

Two days after the Alabama arrived in Cherbourg, Semmes was brought upsetting news. The Union cruiser *Kearsarge*, a black-hulled, steam-powered sloop was steaming at full speed for Cherbourg. Captain John A. Winslow of the *Kearsarge* had been chasing the *Alabama* for almost a year.

The *Kearsarge* arrived off Cherbourg on June 14. Instead of entering the harbor, Captain Winslow took up a position in the English Channel just beyond the 3-mile (5-kilometer) limit, that is, in international waters. There Winslow waited.

Captain Semmes had three choices. He could abandon his ship at the dock. He could steam at full speed out of the harbor, seeking to outrun the *Kearsarge*. Or he could fight. Semmes's choice was to fight. Perhaps hoping to end his career with a dramatic victory, Semmes sailed out to face the *Kearsarge*.

The *Kearsarge* was waiting. Upon sighting the *Alabama*, Captain Winslow took the *Kearsarge* farther out to sea. He wanted to be sure he would not be in French waters when his guns began firing.

Almost 7 miles (11 kilometers) offshore, Winslow suddenly turned and headed straight for the *Alabama*, seeking to run the ship down. Semmes quickly changed course to avoid a collision. The two vessels then found themselves traveling in opposite directions divided by about half a mile of water. The *Alabama* was the first to fire. The *Kearsarge* answered back. In order to keep in range of one another's guns, the two vessels began to steam in a circle.

The *Kearsarge*'s gunners soon showed that they were better trained and disciplined. As shots from the *Alabama* sailed far above their target, a shell from the *Kearsarge* exploded at the stern of the *Alabama*. The blast put a big gun out of commission and killed or wounded half the gun crew. Another shot tore into the *Alabama*'s steering mechanism, crippling the vessel. Fragments from still another shell ripped into Semmes's right hand.

In less than an hour, the powerful guns of the *Kearsarge* had transformed the once proud *Alabama* into a battered hulk. Water came gushing in. In the engine room, steam pressure nosedived. Semmes's only choice was to haul down the ship's flag, a signal of surrender.

Some of the *Alabama*'s crewmen were sent to the *Kearsarge* by lifeboat. They watched with tear-filled eyes as the ship settled beneath the waves, going down stern first. A yacht named the *Deerhound*, which was filled with spectators who had watched the battle, picked up Captain Semmes and forty-one others. They were taken across the English Channel to Southampton.

Gideon Welles was furious that Semmes had managed to escape capture.[5] Semmes later returned to the Confederacy. He was rewarded by being promoted to the rank of admiral and given command of the James River squadron.

The loss of the *Alabama* left the Confederacy with the *Florida* as the only raider on active duty. Like the *Alabama*, the *Florida* had been built in Liverpool,

*For more than an hour, the 11-inch guns of the **Kearsarge** (left) were trained on the **Alabama** (center), battering the vessel and piercing the hull below the waterline. Twenty minutes after Semmes surrendered, the Alabama plunged to the bottom. (Leslie's Famous Leaders and Battle Scenes of the Civil War)*

*With its victory over the **Alabama**, the **Kearsarge** became one of the Navy's most famous ships. This picture was taken in the harbor of Calcutta, India, in the mid–1870s, during an Asian cruise made by the ship.*
(Alberti/Lowe Collection)

neutral nation. But on the night of October 7, the *Florida* was the victim of a sneak attack. Without warning, the Union warship *Wachusett* rammed the *Florida* as it lay at anchor. The crew of the *Wachusett* then took over the Confederate vessel.

While the *Florida* and *Alabama* were among the most noted of eighteen or so raiders put into service by the Confederacy, there were several others that raised the anger of Union military leaders. The *Georgia* is one example. Purchased in Scotland for the Confederates, and commanded by Lieutenant William L. Maury, the *Georgia* sailed from Scotland into the South Atlantic.

While the *Georgia* managed to capture several Union vessels within a short period of time, its career was very brief. The *Georgia*'s failing was its iron hull, which leaked and needed constant attention. It was forced to spend almost as much time in dry dock as at sea. The *Georgia*'s career as a raider lasted only seven months.

England. The vessel captured more than thirty Union merchant ships before coming to an untimely end.

Early in October 1864, the ship dropped anchor in the harbor of Bahia, Brazil. The *Florida*'s captain felt certain that the ship would be safe there, since Brazil was a

The *Shenandoah* was the last of the commerce raiders. Commissioned in 1864, the *Shenandoah* was sent to prey upon the American whaling fleet in the Pacific. Lieutenant James I. Waddell was named to command the vessel.

Cruising as far north as the Bering Sea, the *Shenandoah* captured thirty-eight ships, most of them whalers. The *Shenandoah* thereby almost single-handedly crushed New England's whaling industry.

There is a footnote to the story of the Confederate raiders and the *Alabama*, in particular. In October 1984, a French minesweeper named the *Circe* discovered an unknown wreck in the waters of the English Channel about 6 miles (9 kilometers) offshore from Cherbourg. Scuba divers descended to the site, about 180 feet (55 meters) below the surface. They discovered the wooden hull of a warship. Coal was scattered about, as well as English dishware from the 1800s. Before long, divers were able to confirm that the wreck was that of the *Alabama*.[6]

In the years that followed, divers and underwater archaeologists recovered nails, needles, bullets, lead weights used for taking soundings, and an array of other artifacts from the site. Divers even recovered the *Alabama*'s big Blakely Gun. But archaeologists have decided it would be impossible to lift the *Alabama*'s wooden hull without destroying it. Today, that pile of rotting wood and rusting iron stands as a memorial to the most famous of the Confederate raiders, and the bold though largely unsuccessful effort by the Confederacy to wipe out American commerce and blunt the Union war effort.

Chapter Eight

Sailors in Blue and Gray

Throughout the Civil War, both Union and Confederate navies faced the same problem: There were never enough sailors. The shortage was so severe that warships sometimes put out to sea with incomplete crews. The problem was that the navies had to compete with the armies for the manpower. And it was the armies' demands that were the first to be satisfied.

The Union Navy had an advantage in that it started with a core of experienced seamen and petty officers, enlisted men who had been given command of others. These included gunner's mates; signalmen; carpenters; quartermasters, who handled navigational tasks; and boatswains (pronounced bosuns) mates, whose responsibilities had to do with ship's decks, rigging, anchors, and the like.

There was no Confederate Navy at the beginning of the war. There was thus no pool of experienced men to draw upon. The Union Navy accepted recruits as young as thirteen. In the case of the Confederacy, a boy had to be at least fourteen. In both navies, a boy under twenty-one had to have the consent of a parent or guardian to join.[1]

Before the war, the U.S. Navy, unlike the Army, had permitted blacks to enlist. However, the Navy sought to limit the number of black sailors to one twentieth of the crew aboard a ship. But this restriction was lifted when the Navy's need for sailors became more serious. Toward the end of the war, many ships in the Union Navy had a high percentage of black seamen. Some were former slaves. Slaves were also accepted for ser-

*Boys as young as thirteen were recruited for service in the Union Navy. This boyish teenager was a crew member aboard the **Vermont**, a sailing vessel. (Alberti/Lowe Collection)*

*When the Civil War began, the Union Navy had a core of well-trained and seasoned sailors to call upon, such as this gun crew aboard the steam sloop **Wissahickon**. (National Archives/Mathew Brady Collection)*

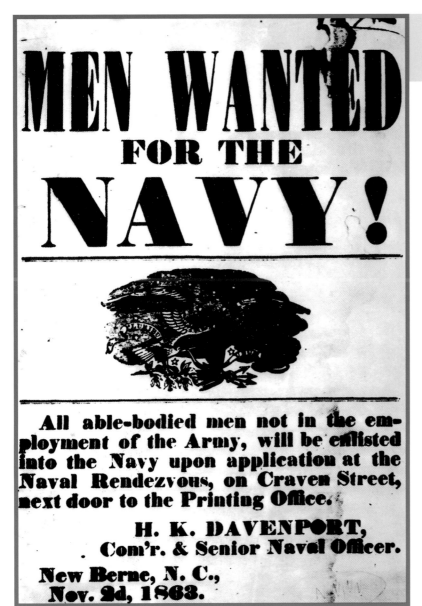

MEN WANTED
FOR THE
NAVY!

All able-bodied men not in the employment of the Army, will be enlisted into the Navy upon application at the Naval Rendezvous, on Craven Street, next door to the Printing Office.

H. K. DAVENPORT,
Com'r. & Senior Naval Officer.

New Berne, N. C.,
Nov. 2d, 1863.

A recruiting poster for the Confederate Navy, issued at New Bern, North Carolina, in 1863. (National Archives)

vice in the Confederate Navy. They first, however, had to get the consent of their owners.

In both navies, sailors were paid the same amounts. An inexperienced seaman was paid $12 a month. What was called an "able-bodied seaman" received $18 a month.

In the Union Navy, "navy blue" was the traditional uniform color. Stephen Mallory, secretary of the navy for the Confederacy, planned to have what he called a "gray Navy." But Mallory's wish was not easy to fulfill. The Confederate Army took most of the gray cloth that was produced by Southern mills. As a result, Mallory's sailors were sometimes issued blue clothing because the Confederates had captured vast stores of blue cloth when they seized the Norfolk Navy Yard early in the war.

In both navies, shipboard life followed the same routine. At 5 A.M. the day began. The boatswain's mate on duty would storm into the berthing compartment, shouting at the sleeping men and rocking their hammocks.

Once a sailor was awake and on his feet, he would immediately roll up his hammock and bedding and lash them into a tight, cylinder-shaped

Crew members of the Union gunboat **Mendota,** *photographed on the James River in 1864, included a good number of African-American and foreign-born seamen. (Author's Collection)*

The boatswain's mate aboard the Union supply ship **New Hampshire** *poses in his dress uniform.* (*Library of Congress/Mathew Brady Collection*)

bundle. On big ships, hammocks were stored on the upper deck, the spar deck.

Once the hammocks were stored, seamen immediately began scrubbing down the ship's open decks. The ship's guns were cleaned. Brass fittings were polished. On large ships, once the ship was cleaned, sailors assembled for inspection by the master-at-arms, a petty officer who kept order aboard the ship. Each man was expected to be clean and neat.

Breakfast followed. Men ate with others of their occupation in groups of eight to fourteen. Each group was called a mess. Coal heavers and the men who tended the boilers had their own mess. So did members of the deck crew. Each man provided his own knife, fork, spoon, and mug.

For breakfast, a sailor might have a mug of black coffee and a strip of salted beef.

*The crew of the **Monitor** lounges about the deck of the famous vessel as the ship's cook prepares the midday meal.*
(Library of Congress/Mathew Brady Collection)

After breakfast, men reported to their duty stations. The deck crew would have scrubbing and painting to do. Gun crews might engage in target practice. Carpenters made repairs to the ship's hull. Belowdecks, engineers tended the boilers and machinery that drove the ship.

Noon brought lunch, the biggest meal of the day. The menu was likely to consist of *hardtack* (hard biscuits or crackers) salted beef or pork, and vegetables. Cheese might also be included. In the case of ships on blockade duty, there were sometimes opportunities to send a small boat ashore to obtain fresh fruits and vegetables. At shore stations, rice and fresh bread might be available.

In the Confederate Navy, each man received one-quarter pound of salted beef, salted pork, or bacon daily. Rice or dried peas or beans were also provided. Coffee and tea were usually available, too, but both became scarce in the final stages of the war.

After the evening meal, crew members relaxed. Men might write letters or read newspapers or books. Checkers, dominoes, and acey-deucey, a form of backgammon, were popular. Gambling was not permitted. On ships fortunate to have a musician or two aboard, the crew might be entertained by a fiddle or banjo.

The Navy's switch from sails to steam power during the Civil War created special strains. Most older officers and crew members didn't like the change. On sailing ships, they had lived outdoors on the open decks. But on the new steam-powered gunboats and monitors, most of their time was spent belowdecks, with the men confined to dark and often sweltering compartments. Candles had to be lit for reading.

When it was sunny and hot, ironclad ships sizzled and the crew sweltered. Sometimes coal smoke filtered belowdecks. Men would head for open hatches to get a breath of fresh air.

Boredom was the Union Navy's biggest problem. For crew members aboard blockading ships, one day followed another with grim monotony, and time dragged. The ship became like a prison. Men could become deeply dejected.

One naval doctor called this "land sickness." Those who had it felt a great urge to see flowers and trees and smell the earth. Sometimes a day or two in port could put an end to the sickness. Other times, a brief change did little to help. Cases of land sickness could bring on serious illnesses.[2]

Despite the problems, sailors of both navies conducted themselves with spirit and courage during the war. In the end the Union Navy proved to be superior. But that was not the fault of the officers and men who served on Confederate ships or at shore stations. The problem was that the South did not have the resources to create a fleet to equal the North's in terms of size or power. From the beginning, the Confederate Navy was in a contest that it could not win.

Chapter Nine

Mobile Bay and Beyond

By the end of 1864, Mobile, Alabama, on the Gulf of Mexico, and Wilmington, North Carolina, were the only ports of any importance still in Confederate hands. Mobile, in particular, was a headache for the Union.

In Mobile Bay, the Confederates maintained a powerful force of gunboats and monitors. For three and a half years, these vessels had managed to frustrate the efforts of Union blockaders to halt ship traffic in and out of the port. The great quantities of war materials being unloaded at Mobile kept the Confederate armies equipped and supplied. Mobile was helping to prolong the war.

The task of closing off the port of Mobile fell to Admiral David Farragut, the hero of New Orleans. It was no easy assignment. Mobile was at the end of long and shallow Mobile Bay at a distance of about 25 miles (40 kilometers) from the bay's entrance. Guarding each side of the entrance were sturdy, heavily armed masonry forts. On the eastern side loomed Fort Gaines, armed with twenty-six guns. Three miles (5 kilometers) to the west, on the other side of the entrance, stood Fort Morgan with forty-five guns.[1] Unfinished Fort Powell, on Tower Island, was smaller, with only six guns.

There was another problem. The Confederates had strewn close to two hundred mines in the channel between the forts. These mines, called torpedoes, were rigged to float just below the surface of the water. Any ship that struck a mine would be blown up.

By mid-June 1864, Farragut had seventeen ships anchored off Mobile Bay, including four big steam sloops. Several monitors were scheduled to join the force.

The Confederate ironclad cruiser **Tennessee** *(left) launches an attack on Admiral Farragut's flagship, the* **Hartford,** *at the Battle of Mobile Bay. (Leslie's Famous Leaders and Battle Scenes of the Civil War)*

squadron could hurry past the forts, their guns blazing, and make it safely into the bay.

As the ships approached Fort Morgan, the fort's guns opened fire. The ships' guns replied. A violent battle unfolded. Cannons boomed and ships shuddered as each gun fired. The sound of shattering wood and the screams and curses of sailors filled the air. A heavy layer of smoke obscured the scene. It was so thick that gunners could hardly see their targets.

Farragut climbed into the ship's main rigging so that he could see over the gun smoke. A sailor put a line around him, lashing him to the mast. This was to prevent him from falling if wounded.

Beyond Fort Morgan, Farragut could see the big ironclad *Tennessee*, one of the most fearful of all Confederate warships. The vessel was commanded by Admi-

While he waited for the monitors, Farragut prepared his ships for the attack. Each large wooden ship was lashed to a gunboat. The gunboats were to act as shields, protecting the wooden ships from cannon fire. They also served as insurance. Should one of the larger ships be disabled, the gunboat to which it was secured would carry it to safety.

About 6 o'clock, on the morning of August 5, 1864, Farragut's ships hauled up their anchors and headed for the entrance to Mobile Bay. Farragut believed that his

Quartermaster James Wood, pictured here at the wheel of the **Hartford,** *in another McPherson & Oliver photograph, received the Medal of Honor for his outstanding performance during the Battle of Mobile Bay. Seaman Joseph Cassier is at Wood's right.*
(Alberti/Lowe Collection)

ral Franklin Buchanan, who had been the captain of the *Virginia* (originally the *Merrimac*). The *Tennessee*'s big guns were ready to hammer the Union ships once they got past the forts. Three Confederate gunboats were stationed farther to the north.

As Farragut looked down, he saw the monitor *Tecumseh* swing out of line and head toward the *Tennessee*. Farragut was puzzled. His orders had been clear. The ships were to steam into the bay without turning or stopping. To do otherwise was to risk destruction by fire from the forts.

Suddenly, the *Tecumseh* shook from stem to stern, then lurched forward. The ship had struck a mine. Water cascaded in through a gaping hole that had been ripped in the ship's wooden bottom. Within seconds, the *Tecumseh* went down, its stern rising out of the water.

Sailors on other ships could see the ship's propeller still turning as it slipped beneath the surface. Ninety-three crewmen lost their lives when the *Tecumseh* went down.

Aboard the *Brooklyn*, lookouts spotted torpedoes just ahead. The *Brooklyn* stopped and began backing hard. Other ships stacked up behind the *Brooklyn*, creating a traffic jam.

"What's wrong there?" Farragut wanted to know.

"Torpedoes! Torpedoes!"

"Damn the torpedoes!" Farragut shouted. "Full speed ahead!"[2]

With that, the order went to the *Hartford's* engine room: "Engines ahead full."

The *Hartford* swung to the port and forged ahead of the *Brooklyn*. The line of ships quickly straightened and followed the *Hartford* beyond the forts and into the bay. Crewmen aboard the Hartford and other ships gasped as they heard mines thud against the sides. But none went off. Apparently their cases had leaked and the powder had gotten wet.

The *Tennessee* and the three gunboats moved to meet Farragut's fleet. But they were hopelessly over-matched. One of the gunboats was captured. Another was beached. The third headed for the safety of Fort Morgan. The *Tennessee* also retired to Fort Morgan.

Farragut ordered the *Hartford* and other ships to anchor in the bay about 4 miles (6 kilometers) north of Fort Morgan. He wanted the crews to have breakfast. Afterward, they would seek out the *Tennessee*.

But then lookouts aboard the *Hartford* reported that the *Tennessee* was steaming toward them. It was true. Admiral Buchanan had decided to make one last desperate attempt to save Mobile Bay.

Farragut could hardly believe his eyes as saw the *Tennessee* approaching. The *Tennessee* was preparing to take on Farragut's entire fleet. "I did not think old Buchanan was such a fool," Farragut said.[3]

Farragut ordered two gunboats, the *Monongahela* and the *Lackawanna*, to intercept the *Tennessee* while the other ships prepared for battle. The *Monongahela* rammed the *Tennessee* on the starboard side, but the ironclad steamed away unharmed. The *Monongahela* suffered a crushed bow.

Then the *Lackawanna* tried ramming *Tennessee's* other side. But the *Lackawanna*, like the *Monongahela*, ended up with a damaged bow. The *Tennessee* was unhurt. Shots and shells from both gunboats bounced off the *Tennessee's* sides.

By now, the *Hartford* was at the scene. The *Hartford's* smoothbores hardly bothered the *Tennessee*. But the *Tennessee's* guns mangled Farragut's flagship, causing many casualties. The *Hartford* limped out of harm's way.

The Union monitors arrived. One of them, the *Manhattan*, was armed with 15-inch (380-millimeter) guns. A booming shot from one of the *Manhattan's* guns crashed through the *Tennessee's* thick armor plate.

Engine trouble forced the *Manhattan* to drop out. But another monitor, the *Chickasaw*, took up the

*The Confederate ironclad **Tennessee** took on Farragut's entire squadron single-handedly at Mobile Bay. The vessel is pictured here after its capture. (Library of Congress/Mathew Brady Collection)*

Beginning in 1862 and continuing until shortly after the Civil War, William D. McPherson and "Oliver" worked as commercial photographers in Baton Rouge, Louisiana, and New Orleans, specializing in *cartes de visite*. They frequently photographed warships and waterfront scenes. They are also known to have made photographs of escaped slaves. These images, and the engravings copied from them, were distributed as antislavery propaganda. McPherson was born in Boston, Massachusetts, about 1833. He worked as a photographer in Concord, Massachusetts, before teaming up with Oliver. After the two men ended their partnership in 1867, Oliver dropped out of sight, while McPherson continued to operate the studio by himself, but not for long; he died that same year in New Orleans.

Farragut's fleet battered the masonry walls of Fort Morgan, causing enormous destruction. (Library of Congress/Mathew Brady Collection/ McPherson & Oliver)

attack. Its 11-inch (279-millimeter) guns blasted away "like a pair of pocket pistols."[4]

Fire from the *Chickasaw* leveled the *Tennessee's* smokestack and destroyed the ship's steering system. Other ships joined in the bombardment from a distance. A shot killed two crewmen aboard the *Tennessee* and broke Admiral Buchanan's leg. He had to be carried belowdecks.

Other shots and shells jammed the portals through which the ship's guns fired. The *Tennessee* was now a hopeless cripple. It could not be steered, and its engines had been put out of action by the loss of its smokestack. Worse, the hull was beginning to leak. Admiral Buchanan had no choice but to surrender. A white flag was thrust up from beneath the deck grating. All firing stopped. The Battle of Mobile Bay was over.

Later in the month, Fort Gaines and Fort Morgan both surrendered. As for the city of Mobile, it remained in Confederate hands until the last month of the war. But with the bay sealed off to blockade-runners, Mobile's value had ended.

Admiral David Porter's fleet off Hampton Roads as it prepared for the attack on Fort Fisher. (Library of Congress/Mathew Brady Collection)

With Mobile Bay in control of the Union, Wilmington, North Carolina, loomed as the next target for the Union Navy. The Confederate port was still a haven for blockade-runners.

Wilmington is located about 40 miles (64 kilometers) up the Cape Fear River from the coast. The key to sealing off the city was Fort Fisher, which had been built on a long and narrow spit of land at the river's mouth. Fort Fisher was, at the time, the strongest fort in the Confederacy.

To take the fort, Admiral David D. Porter assembled a fleet of forty-four ships. These vessels carried a landing force of 1,600 sailors and 400 marines.[5] Porter's plan was for the sailors and marines to attack the fort from the sea side. Army troops were to launch an assault from the opposite direction.

At around midnight on January 12, 1865, Porter's ships began bombarding the fort. For three days and two nights, the shelling continued. Then the troops went into action; hard fighting inside the fort followed. But within a day, Fort Fisher had fallen to the combined Army-Navy force.

Gideon Welles went to President Lincoln to report the Union victory. Lincoln seemed happily surprised.

Admiral David Farragut (left) leans on a cannon aboard the **Hartford** *following his victory at Mobile Bay. With "the great admiral of the war," as he was called, are Captain Percival Drayton (center), Farragut's chief of staff, and Gustavus V. Fox, assistant secretary of the navy. (National Archives/Mathew Brady Collection)*

"Why, there's nothing left for your ships to do," he said.[6] It was true. The Civil War was drawing to a close, and the Navy's role was shrinking. General William T. Sherman had captured Savannah, Georgia, and was driving across the Carolinas. Early in April, General Grant punched through the Confederate defenses at Petersburg, Virginia, and captured Richmond. A week later, on April 9, 1865, Lee surrendered to Grant.

When peace came, both sides could point to their navies with pride. Both the Union and the Confederacy had their share of courageous sailors and bold and determined officers.

But the Confederate Navy did not have the strength to seriously challenge the Union war fleets in size and firepower. It could do little to prevent the blockade from becoming ever tighter. Eventually the South was sealed off from the rest of the world and from the war materials and supplies it needed, a critical factor in the Confederacy's collapse and the surrender of General Lee.

Source Notes

Chapter 1

1. Ross J. Kellbaugh, *Introduction to Civil War Photography* (Gettysburg, PA: Thomas Publications, 1991), p. 19.
2. George Sullivan, *Mathew Brady: His Life and Photographs* (New York: Cobblehill/Dutton, 1994), p. 76.
3. Alan Trachtenberg, *Reading American Photographs* (New York: Hill and Wang, 1989), p. 74.

Chapter 2

1. Fletcher Pratt, *The Compact History of the United States Navy* (New York: Hawthorn Books, 1961), p. 9.
2. Paul H. Silverstone, *Warships of the Civil War Navies* (Annapolis, MD: Naval Institute Press, 1989), p. 13.
3. James Tertius deKay, *Monitor: The Story of the Legendary Civil War Ironclad and the Man Whose Invention Changed the Course of History* (New York: Ballantine Books, 1999), p. 18.
4. Pratt, p. 172.
5. deKay, p. 53.

Chapter 3

1. Ezra J. Warner, *Generals in Blue* (Baton Rouge: Louisiana State University Press, 1964), p. 429.
2. William C. Davis and Bell I. Wiley, *Photographic History of the Civil War*, Volume I, "The Navies Begin" (New York: Black Dog and Leventhal, 1994), p. 219.
3. Bern Anderson, *By Sea and by River: The Naval History of the Civil War* (New York: Da Capo, 1962), p. 37.

Chapter 4

1. Bern Anderson, *By Sea and by River: The Naval History of the Civil War* (New York: Da Capo, 1962), p. 52.
2. Anderson, p. 61.
3. William C. Davis and Bell I. Wiley, *Photographic History of the Civil War*, Volume I, "Strangling the South" (New York: Black Dog and Leventhal, 1994), p. 1004.
4. Davis and Wiley, ibid.

Chapter 5

1. James Tertius deKay, *Monitor: The Story of the Legendary Civil War Ironclad and the Man Whose Invention Changed the Course of History* (New York: Ballantine Books, 1999), p. 36.
2. deKay, p. 122.
3. Bern Anderson, *By Sea and by River: The Naval History of the Civil War* (New York: Da Capo, 1962), p. 72.
4. deKay, p. 127.
5. deKay, p. 177.
6. Paul H. Silverstone, *Warships of the Civil War Navies* (Annapolis, MD: Naval Institute Press, 1989), p. 27.
7. "Underwater Surgery to Save a Historic Warship," *The New York Times*, August 30, 1995, Sec. A, p. 12.

Chapter 6

1. Jack D. Coombe, *Thunder Along the Mississippi: The River Battles That Split the Confederacy* (New York: Bantam Books, 1996), p. 101.
2. Coombe, p. 102.
3. Coombe, pp. 103, 104.
4. William C. Davis and Bell I. Wiley, *Photographic History of the Civil War*, Volume I, "The Conquest of the Mississippi" (New York: Black Dog and Leventhal, 1994), p. 719.
5. Bern Anderson, *By Sea and by River: The Naval History of the Civil War* (New York: Da Capo, 1962), p. 124.

Chapter 7

1. "The Wreck of the C.S.S. *Alabama*," *National Geographic*, December 1994, p. 70.
2. *National Geographic*, p. 73.
3. *National Geographic*, p. 77.
4. *National Geographic*, p. 77.
5. Bern Anderson, *By Sea and by River: The Naval History of the Civil War* (New York: Da Capo, 1962), p. 205.
6. *National Geographic*, p. 67, 69.

Chapter 8

1. William C. Davis and Bell I. Wiley, *Photographic History of the Civil War*, Volume II, "The Sailor's Life" (New York: Black Dog and Leventhal, 1994), p. 361.
2. Davis and Wiley, p. 375.

Chapter 9

1. Bern Anderson, *By Sea and by River: The Naval History of the Civil War* (New York: Da Capo, 1962), p. 235.
2. Fletcher Pratt, *The Compact History of the United States Navy* (New York: Hawthorn Books, 1961), p. 169.
3. Pratt, ibid.
4. Pratt, ibid.
5. Anderson, p. 282.
6. Pratt, p. 172.

Further Reading

Bern Anderson. *By Sea and by River: The Naval History of the Civil War.* New York: Da Capo Press, 1962.

Mark M. Boatner III. *The Civil War Dictionary.* New York: Vintage Books, 1988.

Jack D. Coombe. *Thunder Along the Mississippi: The River Battles That Split the Confederacy.* New York: Bantam Books, 1996.

James Tertius de Kay. *Monitor: The Story of the Legendary Civil War Ironclad and the Man Whose Invention Changed the Course of History.* New York: Ballantine Books, 1999.

Frank R. Donovan. *Ironclads of the Civil War.* New York: American Heritage, 1964.

Christopher Martin. *Damn the Torpedoes: The Story of America's First Admiral, Daniel Glasgow Farragut.* New York: Abelard Schuman, 1970.

John Noel, Jr. *Naval Terms Dictionary.* Annapolis, MD: Naval Institute Press, 1991.

Fletcher Pratt. *The Compact History of the United States Navy.* New York: Hawthorn Books, 1961.

James I. Robertson, Jr. *Civil War! America Becomes One Nation.* New York: Alfred A. Knopf, 1992.

Paul H. Silverstone. *Warships of the Civil War Navies.* Annapolis, MD: Naval Institute Press, 1989.

Index

Page numbers in *italics* refer to illustrations.

D.C. PUBLIC LIBRARY

■■4 6052

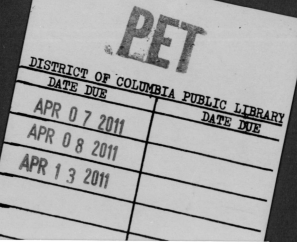

PET

DISTRICT OF COLUMBIA PUBLIC LIBRARY

DATE DUE	DATE DUE
APR 0 7 2011	
APR 0 8 2011	
APR 1 3 2011	

BAKER & TAYLOR

PET
JUV